BYGONE HEATON

Published by Newcastle City Libraries for
Heaton and District Local History
Society.

Published by Newcastle City Libraries
© **City of Newcastle upon Tyne, City Libraries, 1986.**

ISBN 0-902653-34-2

Foreword

This book of photographs showing the Newcastle upon Tyne suburb of Heaton at the turn of the century has been compiled by the Heaton and District Local History Society as an effort to recapture some of the past. Most of the photographs used in the book were taken during the 1910s – a quieter and more peaceful era, and one of great urban expansion.

The photographs used are a selection from the local history collection housed at Heaton Library. We are grateful to the Librarian for allowing us to use them. Our thanks also to Mr. F. Manders and Mr. D. Bond, Local Studies Librarians at Newcastle Central Library for their help and advice.

William Muir.
Chairman, Heaton L.H.S.
1986

Introduction

The name Heaton means "High Settlement" obviously referring to its position high above the river Ouseburn or "Ewes Burn" a glacial tributary of the River Tyne.

The Manor of Heaton was originally part of the Barony of Robert de Gaugy given to him by King John. It later passed into the hands of the Babington family of Harnham in Bolam Parish. Eventually it passed to the Lawson family who sold it to the Ridleys. Richard Ridley built one of Heaton's landmarks, Heaton Hall, in 1713 as a convenient home for the family being in the centre of the collieries owned by them. The original Hall was a plain, square brick building. The two towers and stone facing on the front was added later by Sir Matthew White Ridley.

In 1840 the estate was sold to Mr. Addison Langhorn Potter who was so upset at the run down condition of the estate that he set about restoring it. One of his improvements was to renovate the remains of the 13th century Chapel known as King John's Tower.

The Potter family eventually sold the estate to Lord Armstrong who gave it to the City of Newcastle as a public park. This made a very pleasant walk or carriage ride through three parks for local residents. The Hall remained for a few years more before being demolished to make room for a housing estate called Heaton Hall Estate.

A major access route was, of course, Heaton Road leading from Shields Road to the new Coast Road. During the three decades from 1880 to 1910 this road, including many of the various terraces, avenues and places, was built up as a residential area. Shields Road, a vital east-west link, was, as the name implies the road to Shields. With the construction of Byker Bridge in 1878 the importance of Shields Road as an access route and trading area increased. The tramlines were laid along Heaton Road and Shields Road in 1901 which gives some indication of their importance as access routes even then.

Many of the buildings shown in these photographs have either changed their use or been demolished to make room for more modern buildings.

1. Heaton Hall, built in 1713 by Richard Ridley and improved by Sir Matthew White Ridley. The Hall was demolished early in the twentieth century to make way for residential development.

2. The original Heaton Library, now the Social Services building, was opened as the Victoria Free Library. It was erected by Alderman W. H. Stephenson to commemorate the Diamond Jubilee of Queen Victoria. Earl Grey opened the Library on October 16th 1898.

3. The Park Lodge at the corner of Heaton Park Road and Heaton Park View. The site is
now occupied by the Heaton Library carpark. Today very little of the original iron
fencing remains.

THE PLAYGROUND, HEATON PARK

4. The Playground on the hill in Heaton Park (c1910). Note the remains of the old windmill and the bandstand. The old mill is still extant but the bandstand has been removed.

The Terrace, Heaton Park, Newcastle-on-Tyne

5. The Terrace, Heaton Park, showing the original Pavilion, balustrade and flower beds, with the Bowling Green in the foreground. The Pavilion had now been demolished and rebuilt in Beamish Open Air Museum and a new Pavilion was erected in the Park in 1984.

ST. MARK'S CHURCH, NEWCASTLE.

6. St. Mark's Church, Shields Road. Built on the top of solid sandstone which is only about
   12 inches below the road surface. c1930.

7. The Blue Bell Inn at the east end of Shields Road showing the original turrets, now removed. The opening to the left of the Inn is Byker Hill Square which was removed to widen the road. The chimney belonged to the "Destructor" which burnt household rubbish.

Shields Road, Byker.

8. Shields Road c1910. Note the central tram wires.

HEATON ROAD, NEWCASTLE-ON-TYNE.

9. The corner of Heaton Road and Shields Road looking down Heaton Road. The Chapel on the left is now the site of the Kwik Save Shop. The Trustee Savings Bank, on the right, was originally the Heaton and Byker (Trustees) Savings Bank opened by Sir W. Plummer MP on September 14th 1904.

0. 92   Heaton Road, N C-on-Tyne.

10. Heaton Road looking towards Shields Road. Notice the tramlines and the Newcastle
Co-operative Wholesale Society shop on the right of the picture.

Heaton Road, N C-on-Tyne.

11. Heaton Road looking towards St. Gabriel's Church. On the left are the grounds of
Heaton Hall.

12. The Presbyterian Church on the corner of Heaton Road and Cardigan Terrace.
    Cardigan Terrace is now a bus route. How peaceful it looked in 1910.

TRAM TERMINUS, HEATON, NEWCASTLE-ON-TYNE.

13. The Tram terminus near the Cuthbert Bainbridge Memorial Church. This church was opened on 15th November 1885 to commemorate the work of the Bainbridge Family. The building included school rooms, recreation rooms and offices. A "sewing meeting" used to be held there at which poor women received spiritual guidance and also made clothes from cheap material provided by Bainbridge & Co.

14. Jesmond Vale Terrace was an integral part of Heaton Road facing onto the Park.

15. Mundella Terrace, Heaton is a typical street of late nineteenth century houses. Note the metal railings on the walls. These railings disappeared during the Second World War, melted down for the "war effort".

16. King John Street, Heaton is a typical early twentieth century street of "Tyneside" flats. This type of flat was peculiar to Tyneside. Note the cobble stones which make up the road.

17. A villa on Heaton Park Road now divided into flats.

18. "The Tip" c1910, now the site of the City Stadium and the Ouseburn Community Centre. A track across "The Tip" connected Heaton with Shieldfield. It took many years to infill and many more years to settle before it could be built on.

19. Burnville (1910) leading to Stratford Grove.